EMMANUEL JOSEPH

Innovation vs. Investment, Personal Journeys of Silicon Valley and Real Estate Billionaires

Copyright © 2025 by Emmanuel Joseph

All rights reserved. No part of this publication may be reproduced, stored or transmitted in any form or by any means, electronic, mechanical, photocopying, recording, scanning, or otherwise without written permission from the publisher. It is illegal to copy this book, post it to a website, or distribute it by any other means without permission.

First edition

This book was professionally typeset on Reedsy. Find out more at reedsy.com

Contents

1. Chapter 1 — 1
2. Chapter 1: The Making of a Mogul — 3
3. Chapter 2: Visionaries and Vanguards — 5
4. Chapter 3: The Role of Risk — 6
5. Chapter 4: The Innovation Imperative — 7
6. Chapter 5: Building a Legacy — 8
7. Chapter 6: Mentorship and Influence — 9
8. Chapter 7: The Power of Networks — 10
9. Chapter 8: Balancing Act — 11
10. Chapter 9: The Role of Philanthropy — 12
11. Chapter 10: Lessons Learned — 13
12. Chapter 11: Future Trends — 14
13. Chapter 12: The Legacy of Giants — 15
14. Chapter 13: From Garage to Greatness — 16
15. Chapter 14: The Art of Negotiation — 17
16. Chapter 15: Leveraging Technology — 18
17. Chapter 16: The Global Perspective — 19

1

Chapter 1

Introduction

In the heart of modern economic landscapes, two fields stand out for their extraordinary influence and wealth generation: technology and real estate. These industries have birthed some of the world's most renowned billionaires, each carving their own unique path to success. "Innovation vs. Investment: Personal Journeys of Silicon Valley and Real Estate Billionaires" delves into the captivating stories of these titans, exploring the distinct approaches they took to amass their fortunes and shape their respective domains. This book is an exploration of the diverse roads to success and the powerful forces of innovation and investment that drive these industries forward.

Silicon Valley is a melting pot of ideas, where tech visionaries turn dreams into realities through relentless innovation. This hub of creativity and technological advancement has given rise to household names like Elon Musk, Mark Zuckerberg, and Jeff Bezos. Their journeys are characterized by a daring spirit, a willingness to take colossal risks, and an unyielding drive to disrupt the status quo. The stories of these tech moguls illuminate the relentless pursuit of innovation, the trials and tribulations of startup culture, and the immense rewards of turning a groundbreaking idea into a global empire.

In contrast, the world of real estate is grounded in tangible assets and strategic investments. Real estate billionaires like Donald Trump, Sam Zell, and Barbara Corcoran have built their empires brick by brick, deal by deal. Their success is rooted in a keen understanding of market dynamics, a talent for negotiation, and an ability to foresee and capitalize on emerging trends. The journey of a real estate mogul is one of patience, perseverance, and a deep connection to the physical spaces that shape our urban environments. Through their stories, we gain insights into the art of investment, the significance of location, and the transformative power of real estate development.

Despite their differences, these billionaires share common traits that transcend their industries. Vision, risk-taking, and the ability to navigate uncertainty are hallmarks of their success. They are pioneers who have not only accumulated vast wealth but also left an indelible mark on society. Their journeys offer valuable lessons on the importance of innovation, the power of strategic investment, and the role of resilience in achieving extraordinary success. "Innovation vs. Investment" is not just a collection of individual stories but a broader narrative that highlights the intersecting paths of technology and real estate, and the dynamic interplay between innovation and investment.

As we embark on this journey through the lives of Silicon Valley and real estate billionaires, we will uncover the myriad ways in which they have shaped our world. Their stories are a testament to the human spirit's boundless potential and the transformative impact of visionary leadership. Whether you are an aspiring entrepreneur, an experienced investor, or simply curious about the forces that drive our economy, this book offers a compelling exploration of the paths to success in two of the most influential industries of our time. Welcome to "Innovation vs. Investment: Personal Journeys of Silicon Valley and Real Estate Billionaires."

2

Chapter 1: The Making of a Mogul

Silicon Valley, a place synonymous with innovation and technology, is the crucible where dreams are transformed into billion-dollar realities. The journey of a tech billionaire typically begins with a spark of an idea, often cultivated in a dorm room or garage. It's a tale of audacious ambitions, sleepless nights, and a relentless pursuit of disrupting the status quo. The birthplace of giants like Apple and Google, Silicon Valley is not just a location; it's a state of mind where the impossible becomes possible.

The story of a real estate billionaire, on the other hand, is grounded in the tangible. It begins with an astute eye for opportunity, a knack for negotiation, and a deep understanding of the market's pulse. Real estate moguls build their empires brick by brick, deal by deal. Their journey is one of perseverance, weathering market fluctuations, and making strategic investments that turn undervalued properties into gold mines.

Both paths, though vastly different in nature, require a visionary outlook and a willingness to take risks. The tech mogul sees the world as a canvas of possibilities, where code and creativity can redefine how we live and work. The real estate tycoon views land as a blank slate, capable of being transformed into lucrative ventures that cater to human needs and aspirations.

While one relies on algorithms and digital transformations, the other bets on physical assets and infrastructure. The common thread is the ability to foresee future trends and capitalize on them. For tech entrepreneurs, it's about innovating to stay ahead; for real estate investors, it's about anticipating market shifts and seizing opportunities before they become mainstream.

At their core, both journeys embody the spirit of entrepreneurship—bold, visionary, and relentless in the pursuit of success. These billionaires, whether in the realms of technology or real estate, share an innate drive to shape the world in their image, leaving an indelible mark on society.

3

Chapter 2: Visionaries and Vanguards

In the heart of Silicon Valley, visionaries like Elon Musk and Mark Zuckerberg have transformed their ideas into world-changing enterprises. Musk, with his relentless drive to push the boundaries of space exploration and electric vehicles, exemplifies the spirit of innovation. His journey from PayPal to SpaceX and Tesla is a testament to his unyielding belief in the power of technology to solve humanity's greatest challenges. Similarly, Zuckerberg's creation of Facebook redefined how we connect and share information, turning social networking into a global phenomenon.

In the realm of real estate, figures like Donald Trump and Sam Zell have carved their own paths to success. Trump's flamboyant style and high-profile deals have made him a household name, while Zell's shrewd investments and ability to foresee market trends have earned him the moniker "The Grave Dancer." Both have leveraged their keen business acumen to build vast empires, transforming skylines and redefining urban landscapes.

These billionaires, though operating in different industries, share a common trait: the ability to envision a future that others cannot see. They are vanguards, leading the charge in their respective fields and inspiring others to follow in their footsteps. Their journeys are marked by bold decisions, calculated risks, and an unwavering commitment to their visions.

4

Chapter 3: The Role of Risk

The road to becoming a billionaire is fraught with risks. For tech entrepreneurs, the risk lies in the uncharted territory of innovation. Creating something new involves countless unknowns, from technical challenges to market acceptance. The story of Steve Jobs and Apple is a prime example. Jobs risked everything to launch the Macintosh, a gamble that ultimately paid off and revolutionized personal computing.

Real estate investors face a different set of risks. Market fluctuations, economic downturns, and changes in regulatory environments can all impact the value of their investments. The 2008 financial crisis is a stark reminder of these risks, as many real estate moguls saw their fortunes plummet. However, those who navigated the crisis with foresight and resilience, like Warren Buffett, emerged stronger and more successful.

Risk-taking is an essential part of the journey for both tech moguls and real estate tycoons. It requires a combination of intuition, knowledge, and a willingness to embrace failure as a stepping stone to success. The ability to manage and mitigate risk is what sets these billionaires apart from others who falter along the way.

5

Chapter 4: The Innovation Imperative

Innovation is the lifeblood of Silicon Valley. The relentless pursuit of new ideas and technologies drives the region's success. Companies like Google and Amazon have thrived by constantly innovating and adapting to changing market demands. Google's foray into artificial intelligence and Amazon's expansion into cloud computing are prime examples of how innovation can create new revenue streams and fuel growth.

For real estate investors, innovation takes a different form. It involves finding creative ways to add value to properties and identifying emerging trends in urban development. Green building practices, mixed-use developments, and smart city technologies are some of the innovations that have transformed the real estate landscape. Visionary investors like Peter Thiel have recognized the potential of such innovations and capitalized on them to build successful portfolios.

Whether in technology or real estate, innovation is key to staying ahead of the competition. It requires a forward-thinking mindset and a willingness to challenge conventional wisdom. Those who embrace innovation are better positioned to capitalize on new opportunities and achieve long-term success.

6

Chapter 5: Building a Legacy

For many billionaires, the ultimate goal is to build a lasting legacy. In Silicon Valley, this often means creating products and services that have a profound impact on society. Bill Gates, through Microsoft and the Bill & Melinda Gates Foundation, has left an indelible mark on both the tech industry and global philanthropy. His efforts to eradicate diseases and improve education have touched millions of lives.

In the world of real estate, legacy-building often involves transforming communities and leaving a lasting architectural imprint. Developers like Stephen Ross, the mastermind behind New York's Hudson Yards, have redefined urban living and set new standards for mixed-use developments. Their projects not only generate financial returns but also create vibrant, sustainable communities that enhance the quality of life for residents.

Building a legacy requires a long-term perspective and a commitment to making a positive impact. It goes beyond personal wealth and success, encompassing a vision for a better future. Billionaires who prioritize legacy-building are often driven by a deep sense of purpose and a desire to leave the world a better place than they found it.

Chapter 6: Mentorship and Influence

Billionaires often play a crucial role in shaping the next generation of entrepreneurs. In Silicon Valley, mentorship is a cornerstone of the ecosystem. Icons like Steve Jobs and Bill Gates have inspired countless young innovators through their journeys and insights. Programs like Y Combinator and accelerators provide valuable mentorship, funding, and resources to help startups navigate the challenging early stages.

In the real estate world, mentorship takes on a different form. Veteran investors like Barbara Corcoran and Robert Kiyosaki have shared their wisdom through books, seminars, and television shows. Their teachings emphasize the importance of financial education, strategic thinking, and the power of real estate as a wealth-building tool.

The influence of these billionaires extends beyond their immediate circles. They shape industries, set trends, and inspire others to pursue their dreams. Whether through direct mentorship or by serving as role models, their impact is profound and far-reaching.

8

Chapter 7: The Power of Networks

Success in both technology and real estate is often built on strong networks. In Silicon Valley, connections to venture capitalists, engineers, and fellow entrepreneurs can make or break a startup. The culture of collaboration and knowledge-sharing is a key driver of innovation. Events like TechCrunch Disrupt and the Consumer Electronics Show (CES) provide platforms for networking, learning, and showcasing new ideas.

Real estate investors also rely heavily on their networks. Relationships with brokers, contractors, and other investors can provide valuable insights and opportunities. Real estate clubs, industry conferences, and online forums facilitate the exchange of knowledge and deal-making.

Building and maintaining a robust network requires effort, trust, and reciprocity. Billionaires who excel in this area understand the value of fostering relationships and leveraging their networks to achieve mutual success.

9

Chapter 8: Balancing Act

Achieving billionaire status often comes at a cost. The demands of building and maintaining an empire can take a toll on personal relationships, health, and well-being. Silicon Valley moguls like Jeff Bezos and Elon Musk have faced public scrutiny over their work-life balance, as their relentless drive for success often leads to long hours and high stress.

Real estate moguls face similar challenges. The constant need to manage properties, negotiate deals, and stay ahead of market trends can be all-consuming. Balancing family life, health, and personal interests with business demands requires discipline and intentionality.

Despite these challenges, many billionaires find ways to achieve balance. Some, like Richard Branson, emphasize the importance of work-life integration and prioritize time for personal pursuits and adventures. Others adopt practices like mindfulness, exercise, and delegation to manage stress and maintain well-being.

10

Chapter 9: The Role of Philanthropy

Philanthropy is a common thread among many billionaires. In Silicon Valley, the wealth generated by tech giants has led to significant philanthropic efforts. The Giving Pledge, initiated by Warren Buffett and Bill Gates, encourages billionaires to commit a majority of their wealth to charitable causes. Tech moguls like Zuckerberg and his wife, Priscilla Chan, have launched initiatives focused on education, healthcare, and scientific research.

Real estate billionaires also engage in philanthropy, often focusing on community development and social issues. Organizations like the Tony Elumelu Foundation and the Oprah Winfrey Foundation provide support for entrepreneurship, education, and empowerment.

Philanthropy allows billionaires to give back to society, address pressing issues, and create a positive impact. It reflects their values and legacy, showcasing their commitment to making the world a better place.

11

Chapter 10: Lessons Learned

The journeys of Silicon Valley and real estate billionaires offer valuable lessons for aspiring entrepreneurs. Persistence, resilience, and the ability to adapt are key traits shared by these successful individuals. Failures and setbacks are viewed as opportunities for growth and learning.

Both tech moguls and real estate tycoons emphasize the importance of vision, risk-taking, and innovation. They encourage aspiring entrepreneurs to dream big, think creatively, and pursue their passions with unwavering determination.

Networking, mentorship, and continuous learning are also critical components of success. Building strong relationships, seeking guidance from experienced mentors, and staying informed about industry trends can provide a competitive edge.

12

Chapter 11: Future Trends

The landscape of both technology and real estate is constantly evolving. Emerging technologies like artificial intelligence, blockchain, and renewable energy are shaping the future of Silicon Valley. Companies that embrace these innovations are poised to lead the next wave of disruption.

In real estate, trends like sustainable development, smart cities, and co-living spaces are transforming the industry. Investors who recognize and capitalize on these trends can achieve significant success and impact.

Billionaires in both fields must stay ahead of the curve, continually seeking new opportunities and adapting to changing market dynamics. The ability to anticipate and respond to future trends is crucial for sustained success.

13

Chapter 12: The Legacy of Giants

The legacy of Silicon Valley and real estate billionaires is one of transformation, innovation, and impact. Their journeys inspire countless individuals to pursue their own entrepreneurial dreams and strive for greatness.

Through their achievements, they have reshaped industries, improved lives, and left an indelible mark on the world. Their stories remind us of the power of vision, determination, and the human spirit to achieve the extraordinary.

As we look to the future, the legacies of these giants will continue to inspire and guide the next generation of innovators and investors. Their contributions serve as a testament to the boundless potential of human ingenuity and the enduring impact of entrepreneurship.

14

Chapter 13: From Garage to Greatness

The lore of Silicon Valley is filled with stories of humble beginnings. Many of today's tech giants started in garages or tiny apartments, fueled by little more than passion and vision. Steve Wozniak and Steve Jobs of Apple, Larry Page and Sergey Brin of Google, and Jeff Bezos of Amazon all exemplify how revolutionary ideas can take root in the most unassuming places. These startups faced early struggles, financial constraints, and skepticism, but their unwavering belief in their mission propelled them forward.

In real estate, the journey often starts with a single property or a small investment. Real estate mogul Harry Helmsley began his career as a property manager before building a multi-billion-dollar empire. The initial challenges of navigating the market, securing financing, and managing properties laid the foundation for his future success.

These origin stories highlight the importance of perseverance, resourcefulness, and the ability to see potential where others do not. They remind us that great things can come from modest beginnings, and that the journey to greatness often involves overcoming significant obstacles.

15

Chapter 14: The Art of Negotiation

Negotiation is a critical skill for both tech entrepreneurs and real estate investors. In Silicon Valley, securing funding, partnerships, and acquisitions often hinges on effective negotiation. Founders must be able to articulate their vision, demonstrate value, and build trust with investors and partners. Elon Musk's negotiations with NASA and private investors for SpaceX showcase the power of negotiation in turning ambitious projects into reality.

In real estate, negotiation is an everyday necessity. Successful investors negotiate property purchases, lease agreements, and financing terms. Donald Trump's career is marked by high-stakes negotiations, from acquiring prime real estate to securing financing for major developments. The ability to negotiate favorable terms can significantly impact the profitability and success of real estate ventures.

Mastering the art of negotiation requires preparation, patience, and the ability to understand and align with the interests of the other party. It is a skill that can be honed and developed over time, and one that is essential for achieving success in both technology and real estate.

16

Chapter 15: Leveraging Technology

Technology is the driving force behind Silicon Valley's success, but it also plays a crucial role in modern real estate. Tech entrepreneurs harness the power of software, hardware, and data to create innovative solutions that address pressing problems. From cloud computing to artificial intelligence, technology is at the heart of the digital revolution.

Real estate investors are also leveraging technology to transform the industry. Proptech, or property technology, encompasses a range of innovations that enhance property management, streamline transactions, and improve the overall efficiency of real estate operations. Virtual tours, blockchain-based property records, and smart home technologies are just a few examples of how technology is reshaping real estate.

Embracing technology allows both tech entrepreneurs and real estate investors to stay competitive and adapt to changing market dynamics. It opens up new possibilities, enhances decision-making, and creates opportunities for growth and innovation.

17

Chapter 16: The Global Perspective

While Silicon Valley and real estate hotspots like New York and London are renowned, billionaires in these fields often operate on a global scale. Tech companies like Google, Facebook, and Amazon have a worldwide presence, impacting markets and lives across the globe. Their products and services transcend geographical boundaries, driving global connectivity and economic growth.

Real estate billionaires also invest globally, seeking opportunities in emerging markets and major cities around the world. Investors like Li Ka-Shing and Gerald Grosvenor have built diversified portfolios that span continents. Global investments require a deep understanding of local markets, regulations, and cultural nuances.

The ability to think and act globally is a hallmark of successful billionaires. It allows them to tap into a wider range of opportunities, mitigate risks through diversification, and make a broader impact.

Innovation vs. Investment: Personal Journeys of Silicon Valley and Real Estate Billionaires

In the dynamic and ever-evolving worlds of technology and real estate, there are those who stand at the pinnacle, having navigated the twists and turns of entrepreneurship to amass fortunes and transform industries. "Innovation vs. Investment" takes readers on an illuminating journey into the lives of some of the most influential billionaires in Silicon Valley and the real estate sector.

This book delves deep into the personal stories of visionary tech moguls and astute real estate tycoons, exploring the stark contrasts and surprising similarities in their paths to success. From the birth of groundbreaking ideas in a Silicon Valley garage to the strategic acquisition of prime properties, each chapter unveils the unique challenges and triumphs faced by these industry giants.

Through a blend of engaging narrative and insightful analysis, "Innovation vs. Investment" captures the essence of what it takes to build an empire. Readers will discover the power of innovation, the importance of risk-taking, and the value of mentorship and networks. The book also sheds light on the balancing act between personal life and business, the role of philanthropy, and the enduring legacies left by these extraordinary individuals.

Whether you are an aspiring entrepreneur, a seasoned investor, or simply fascinated by the stories of those who shape our world, this book offers valuable lessons and inspiration. "Innovation vs. Investment" is a compelling read that celebrates the relentless spirit of entrepreneurship and the remarkable achievements of Silicon Valley and real estate billionaires.

www.ingramcontent.com/pod-product-compliance
Lightning Source LLC
LaVergne TN
LVHW010445070526
838199LV00066B/6215